Swearing Word

Mr. J Norwell

Stress Relief Coloring Book Flowers

Adult Coloring Book

Published by PUBLISHING COMPANY in 2016
First edition: First printing
Illustrations and design © 2016 Adult Coloring Book J. Kaiwell

allcoloringbook.com

ISBN-13: 978-1530182350
ISBN-10: 1530182352

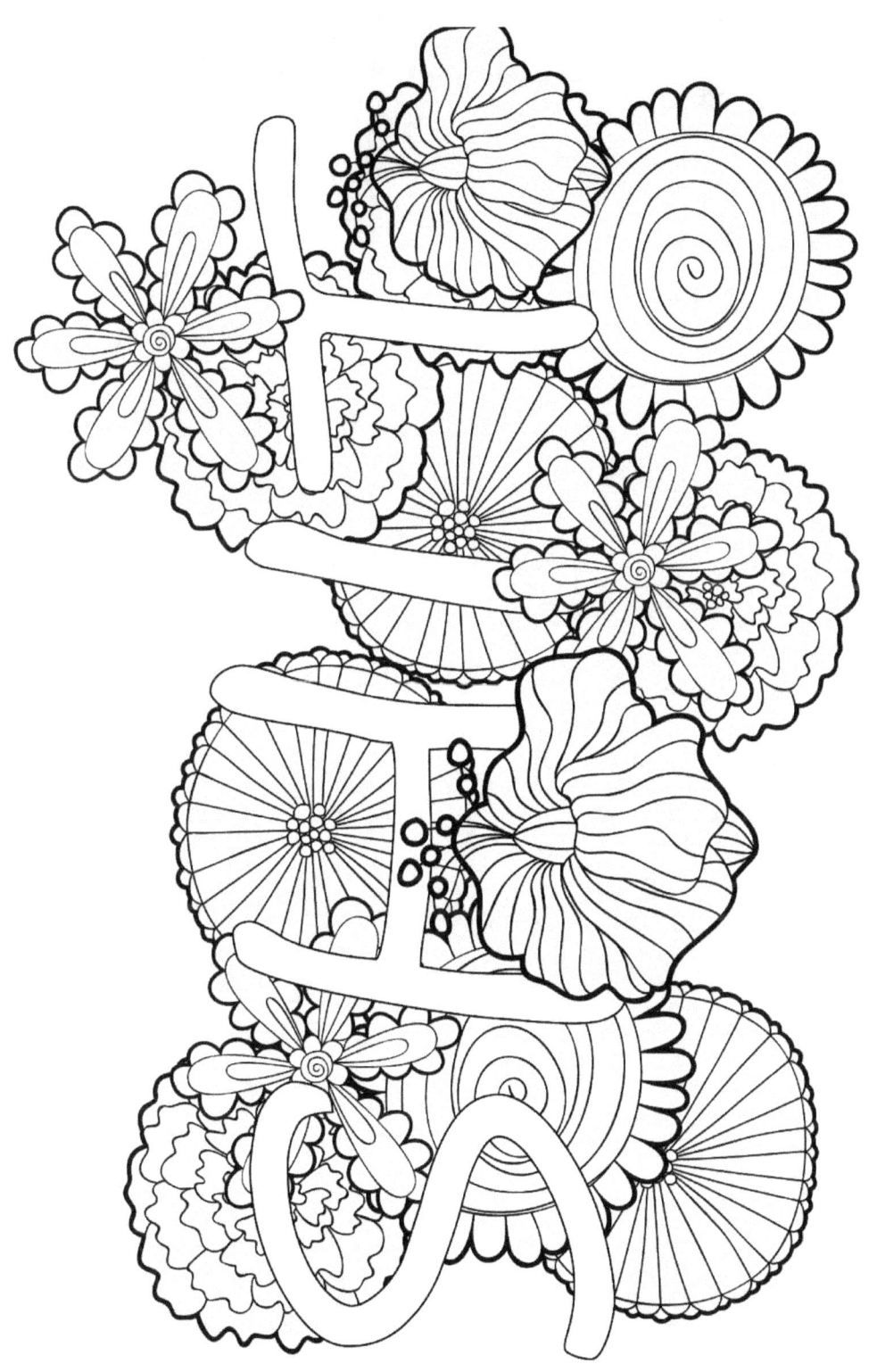

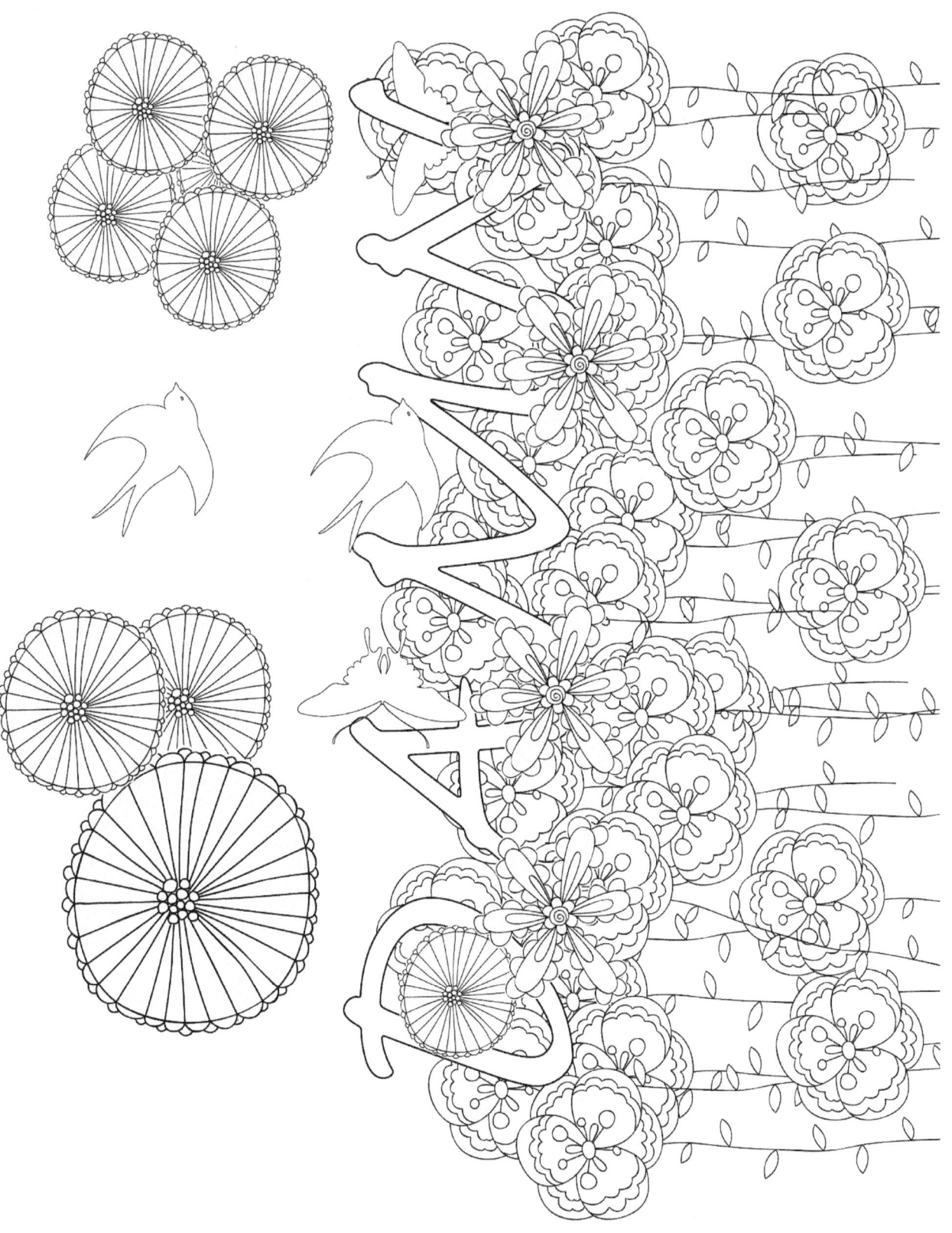

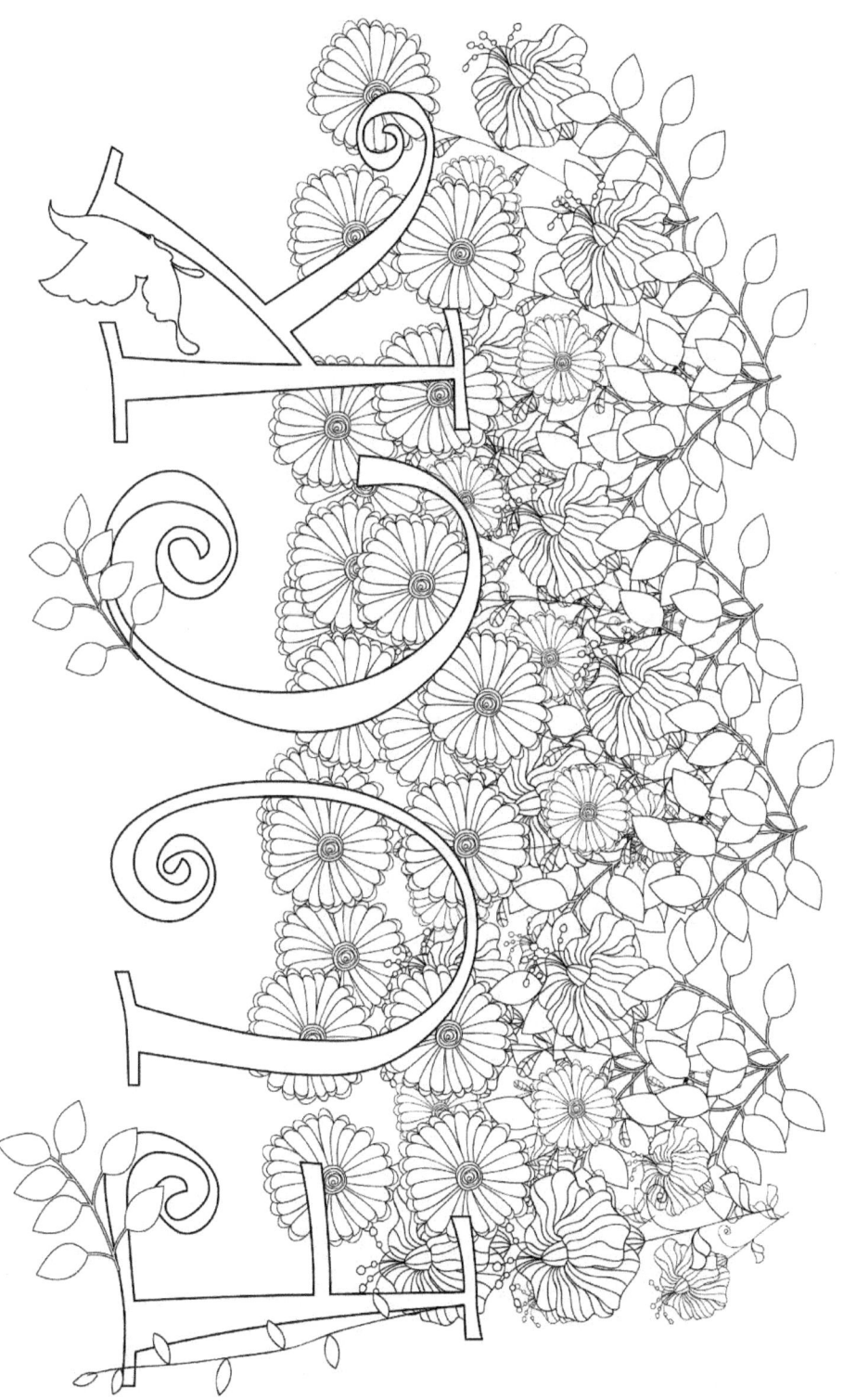

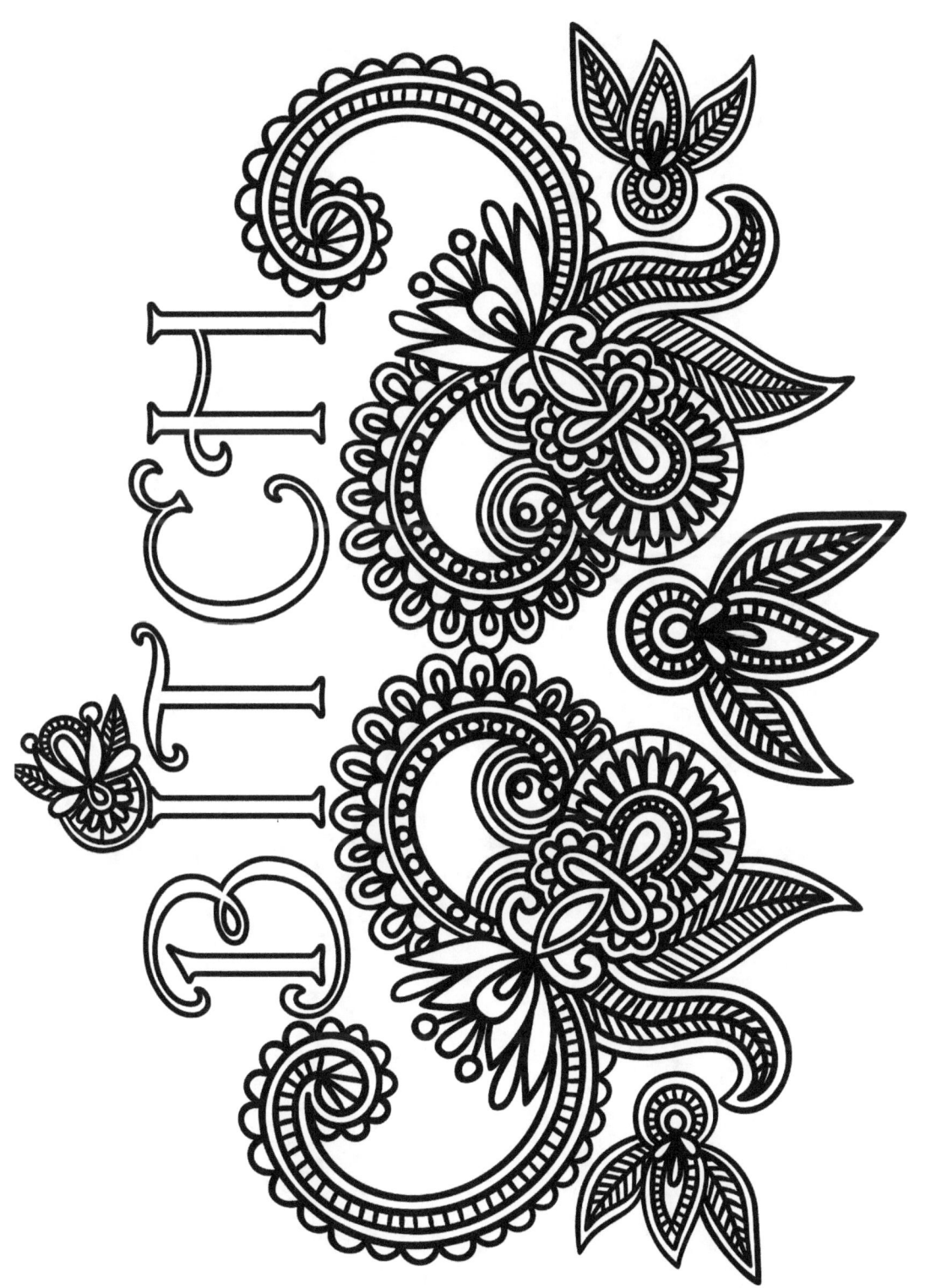

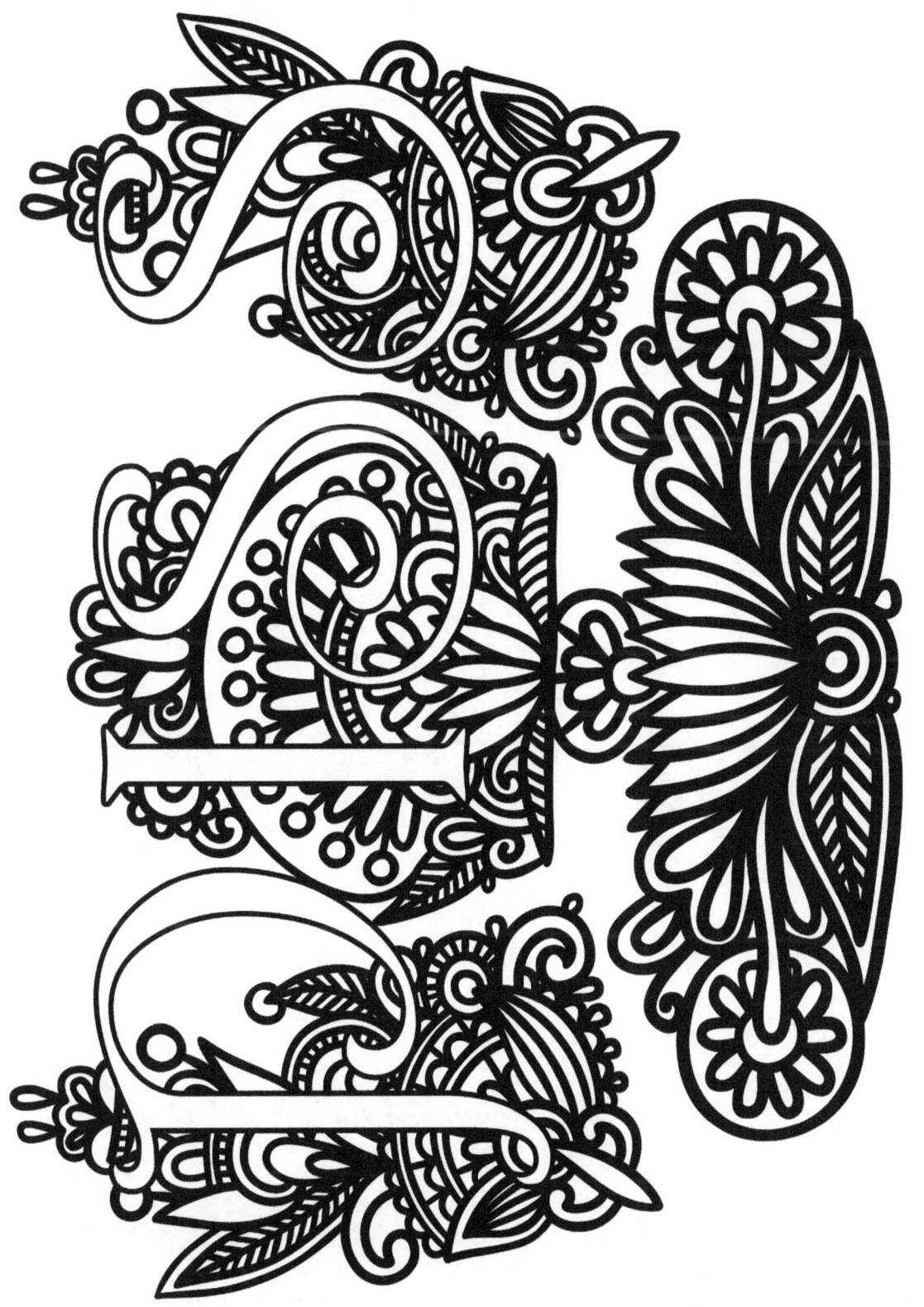

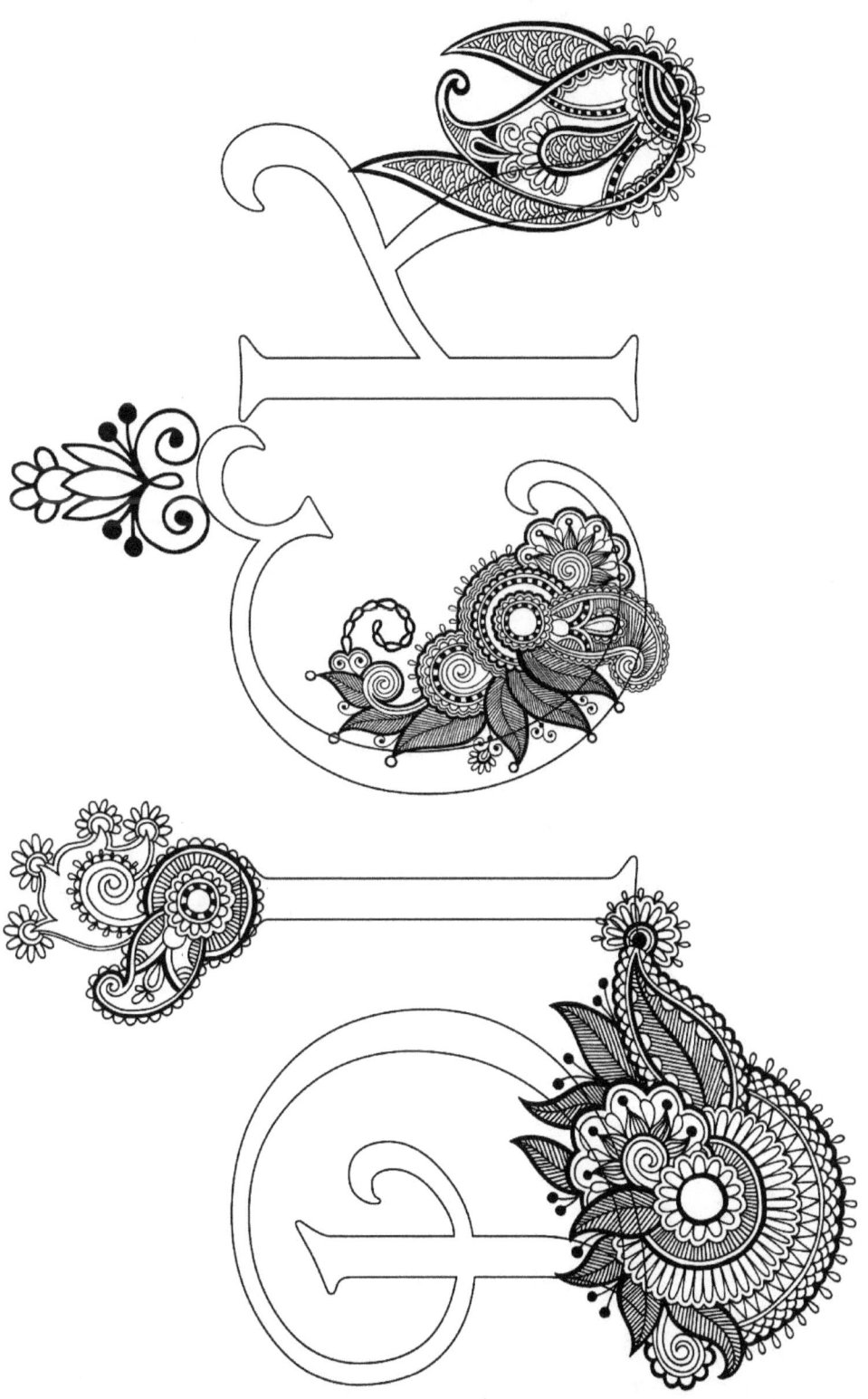

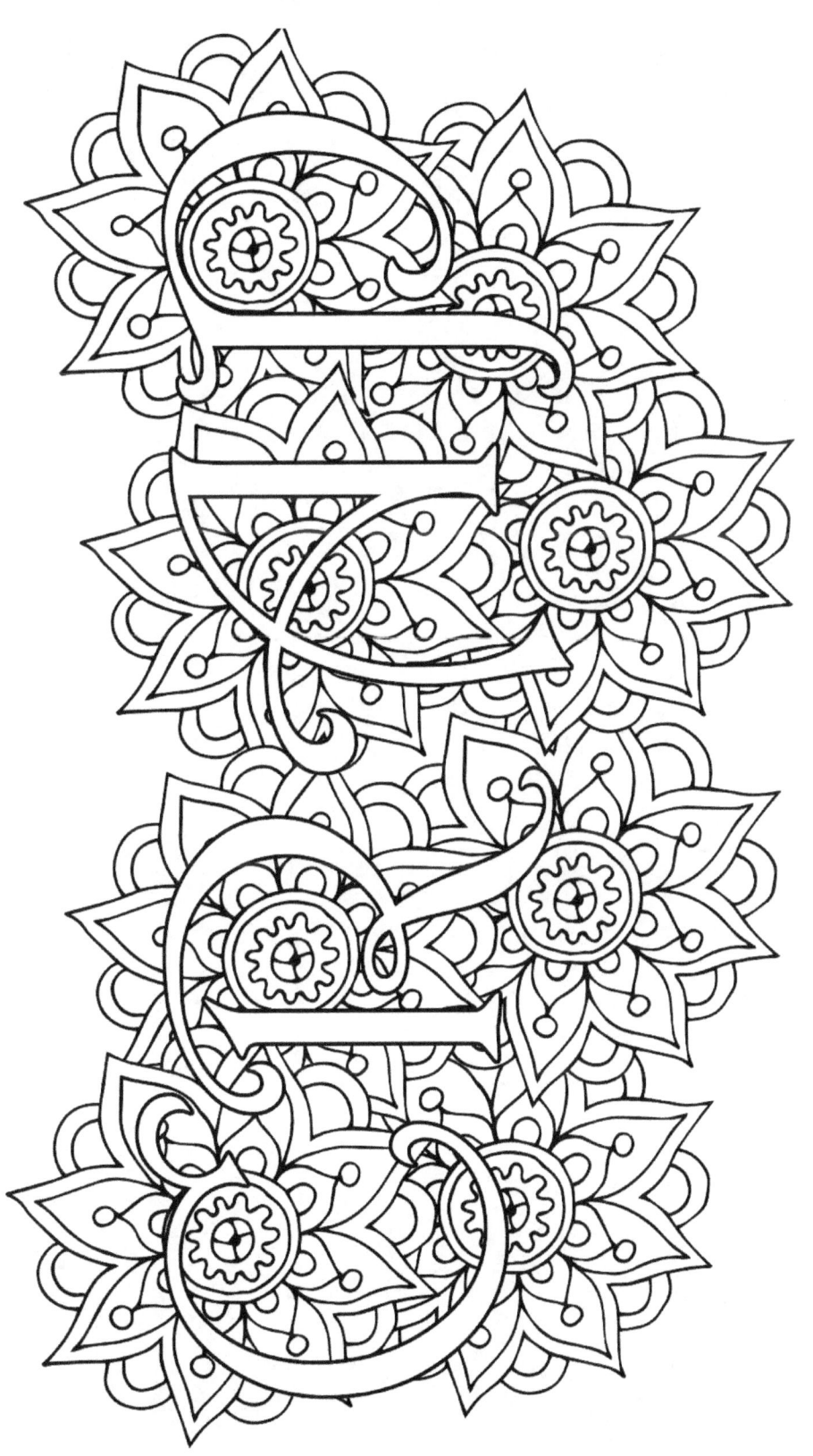

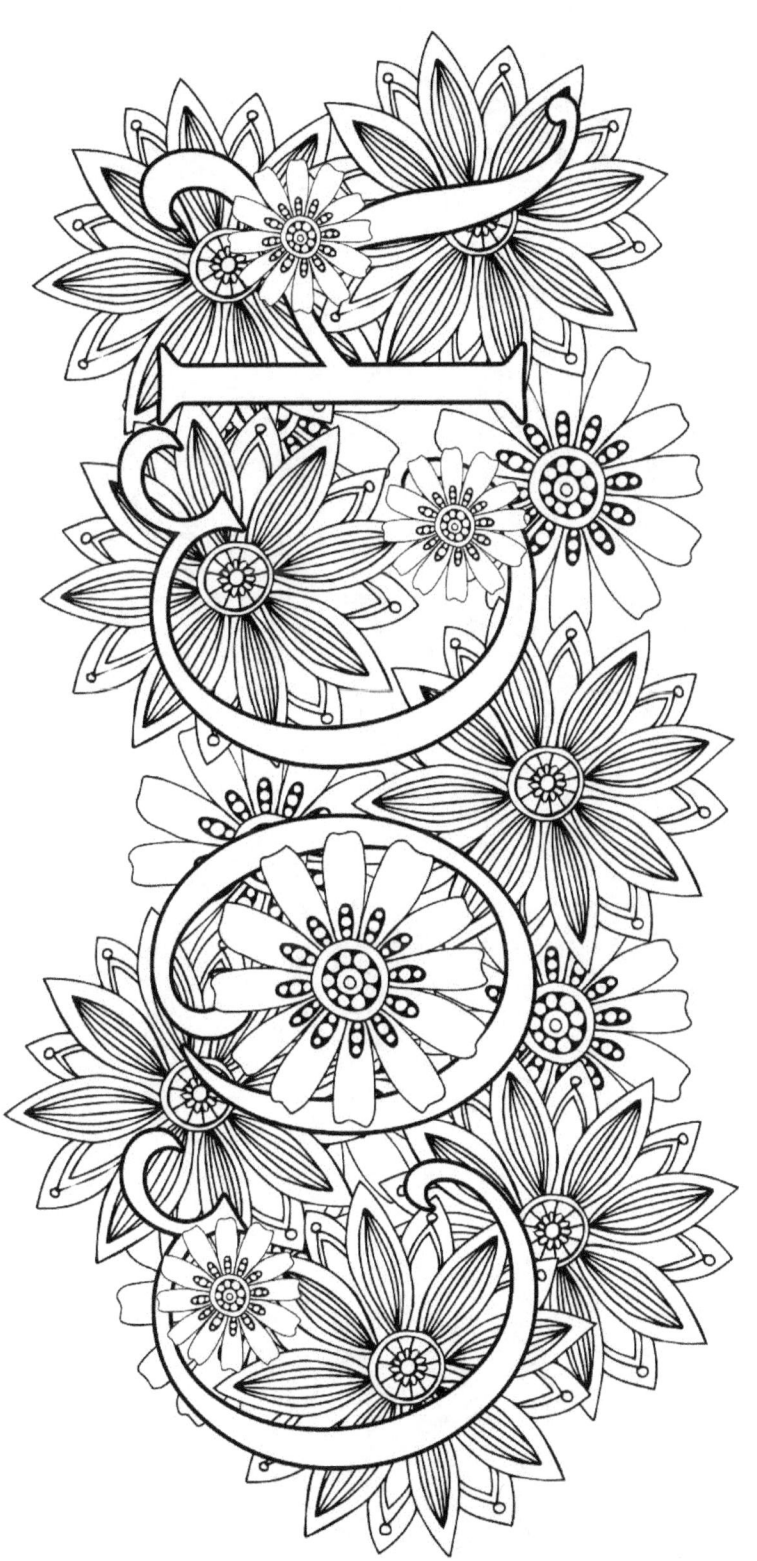

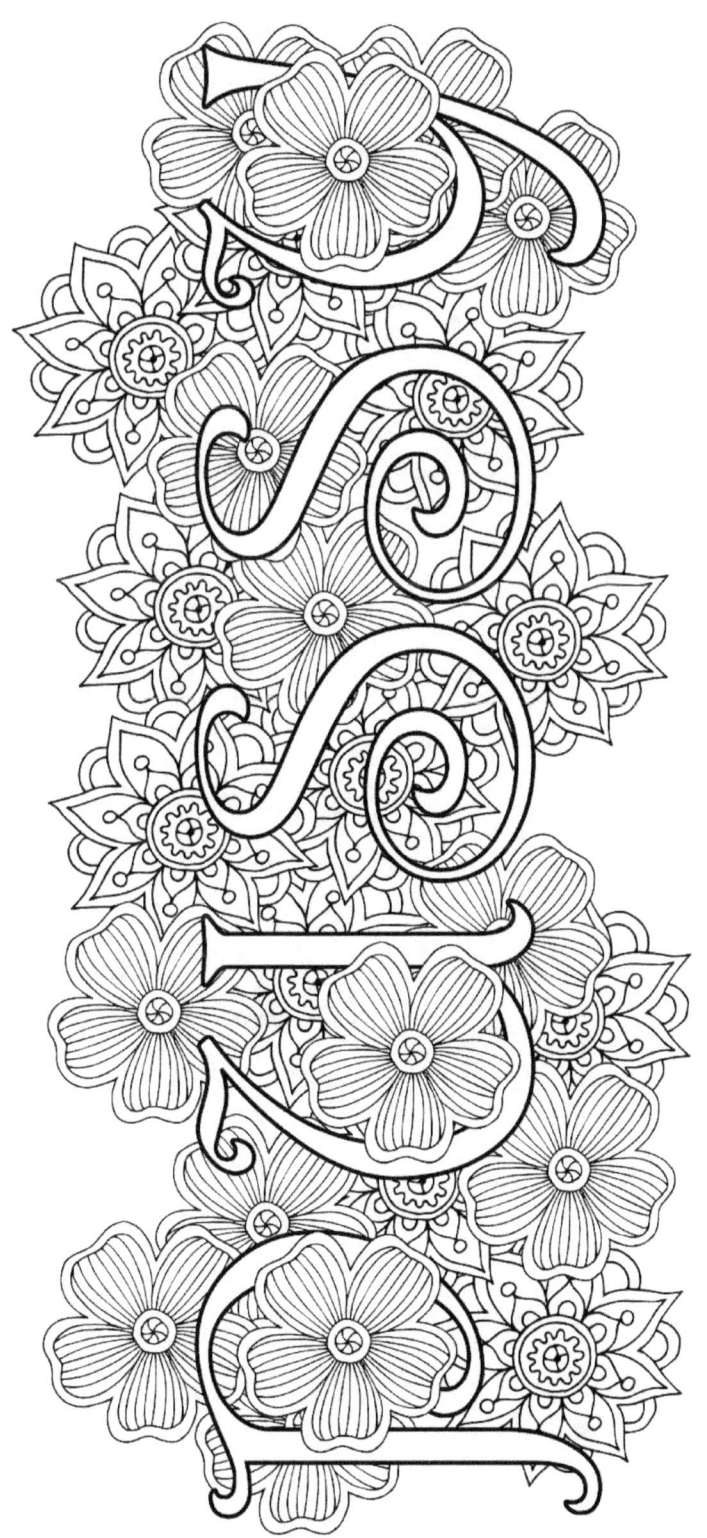

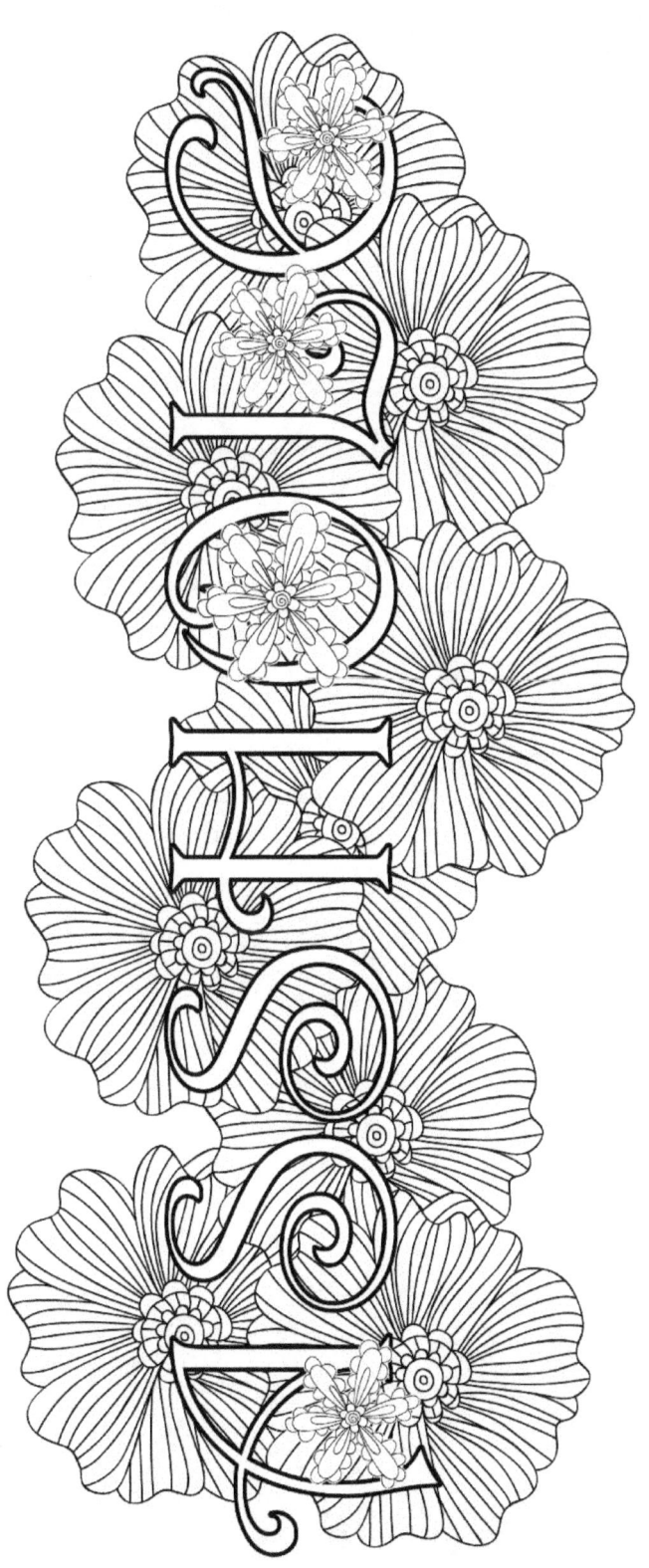

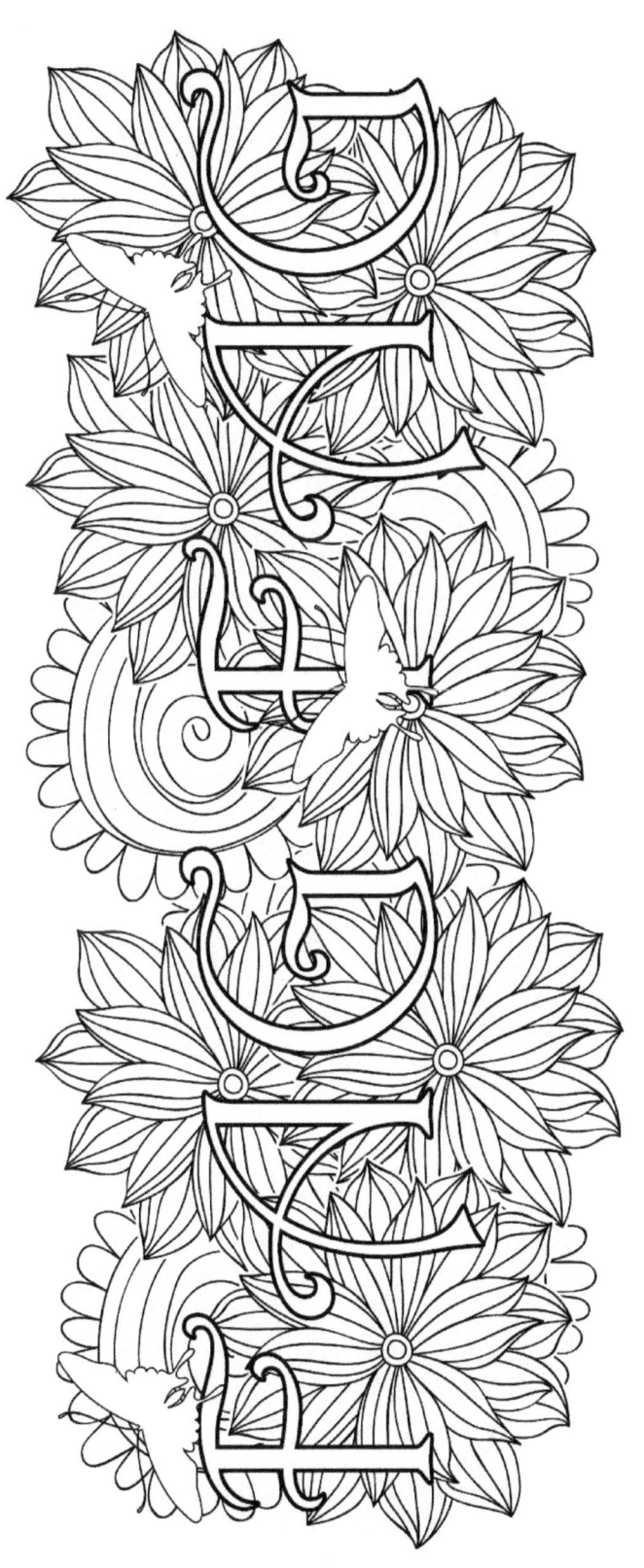

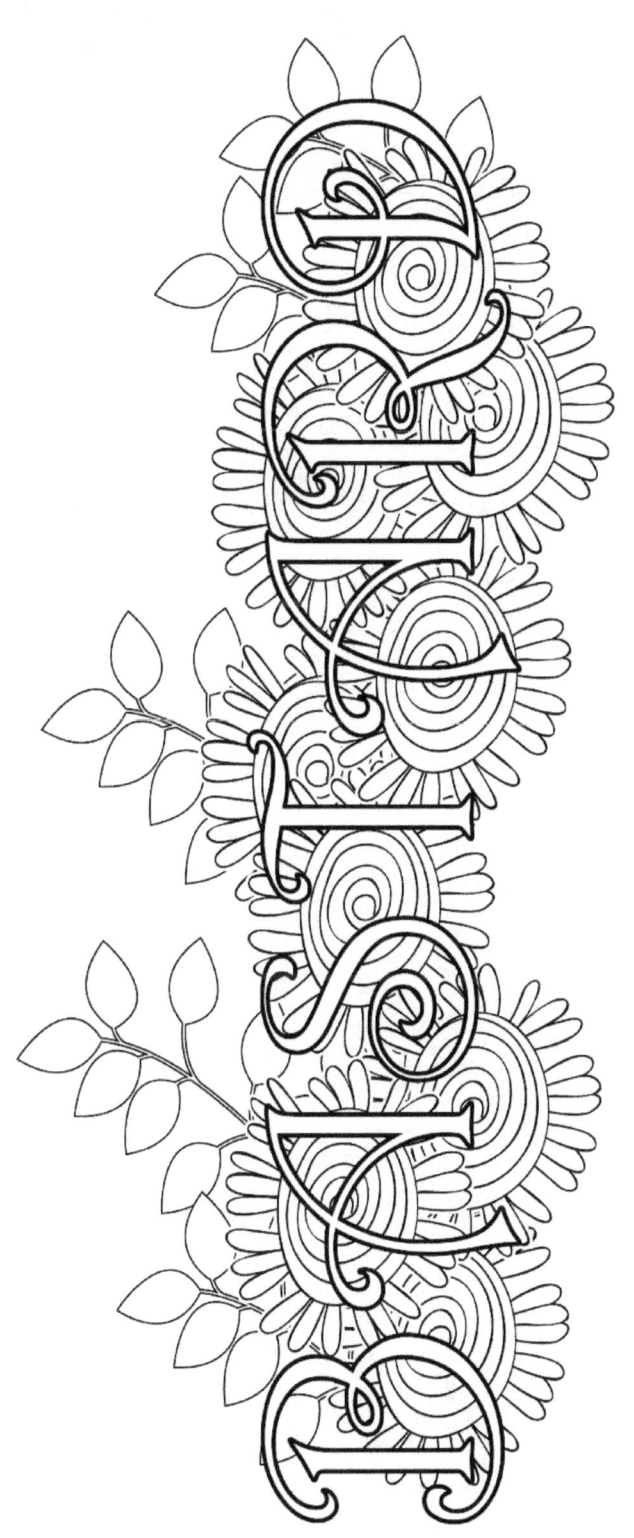

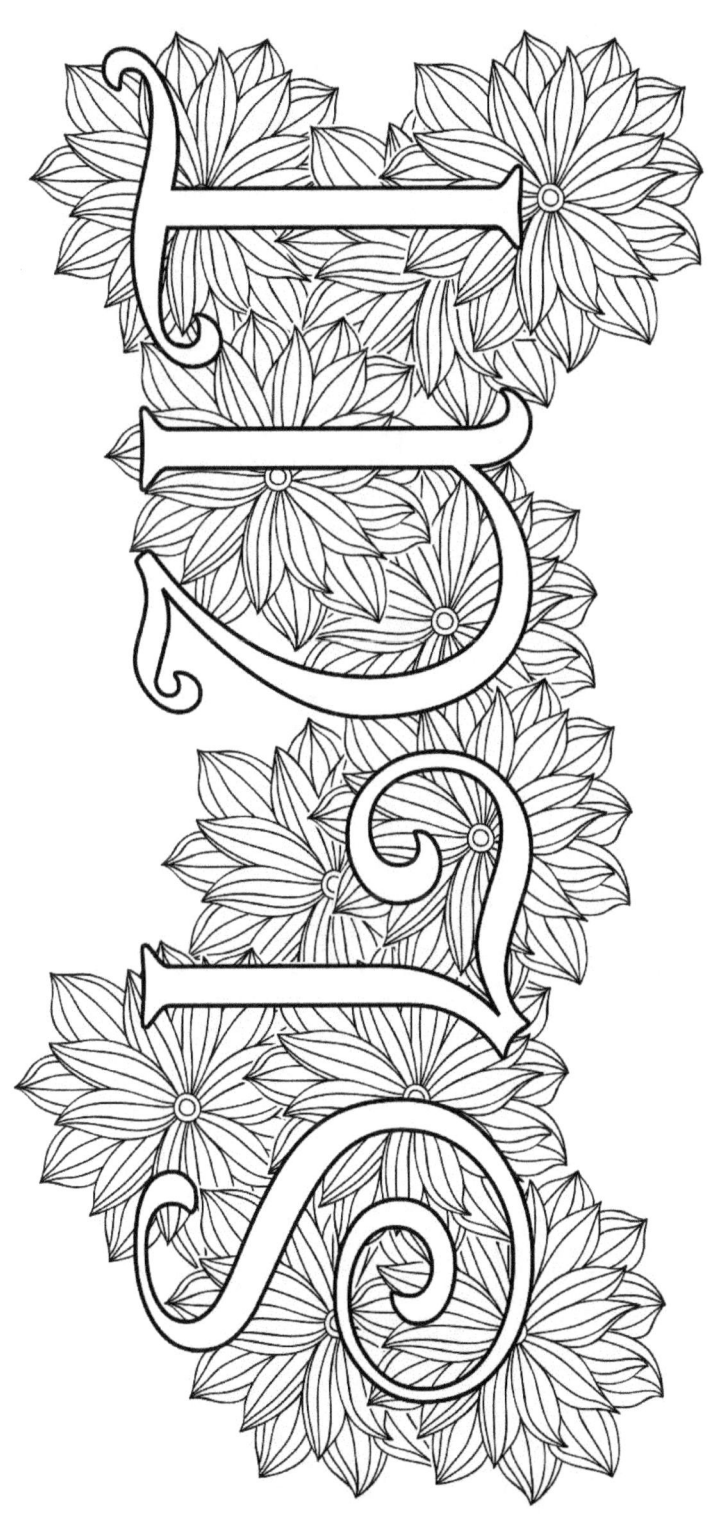

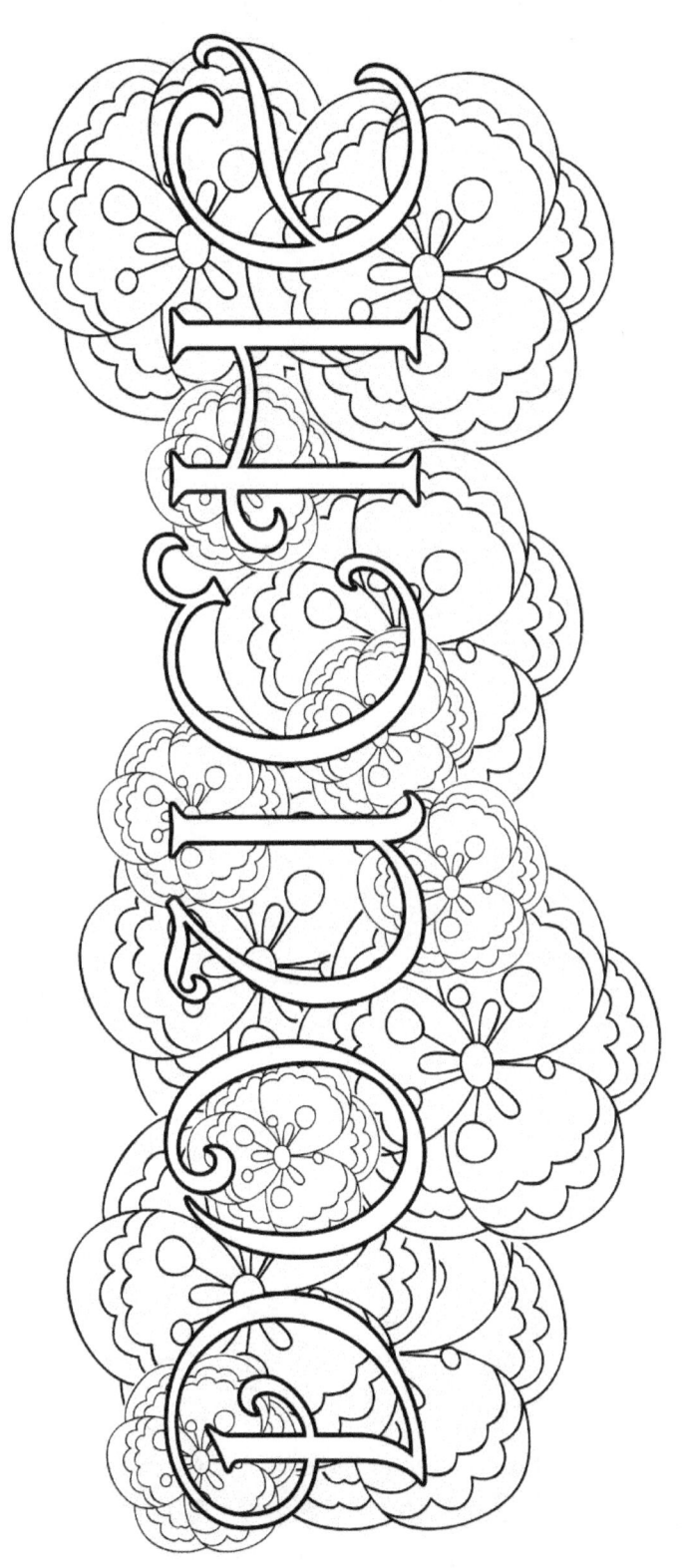

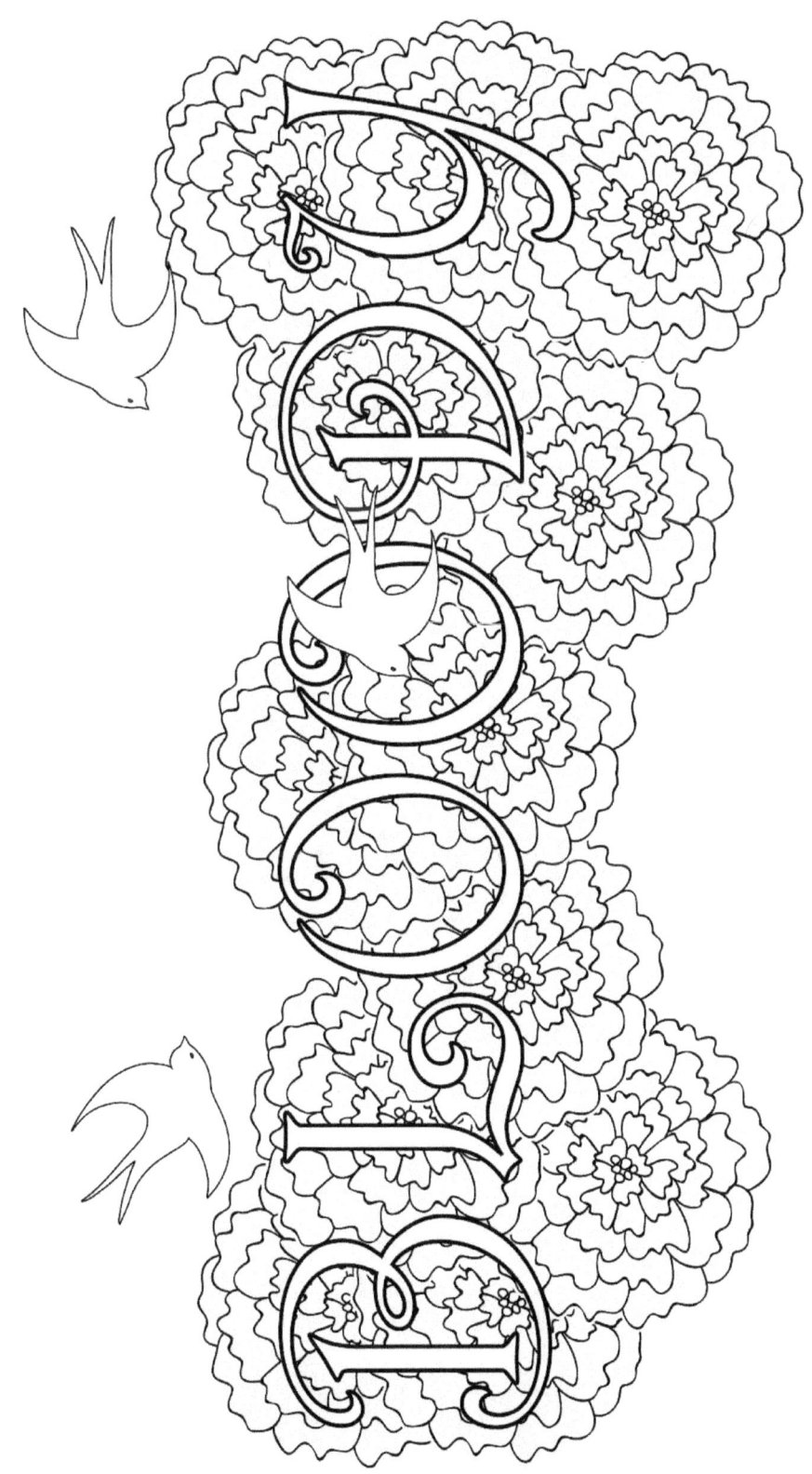

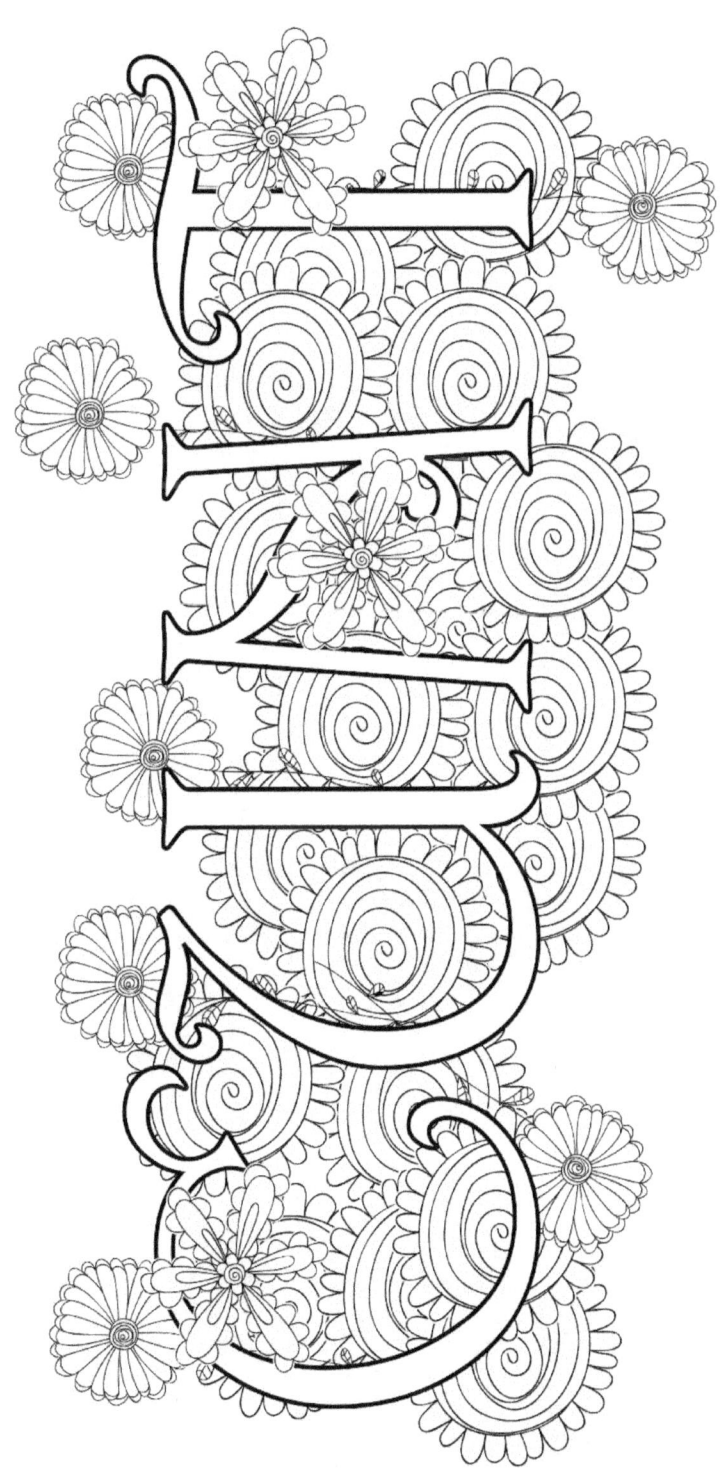

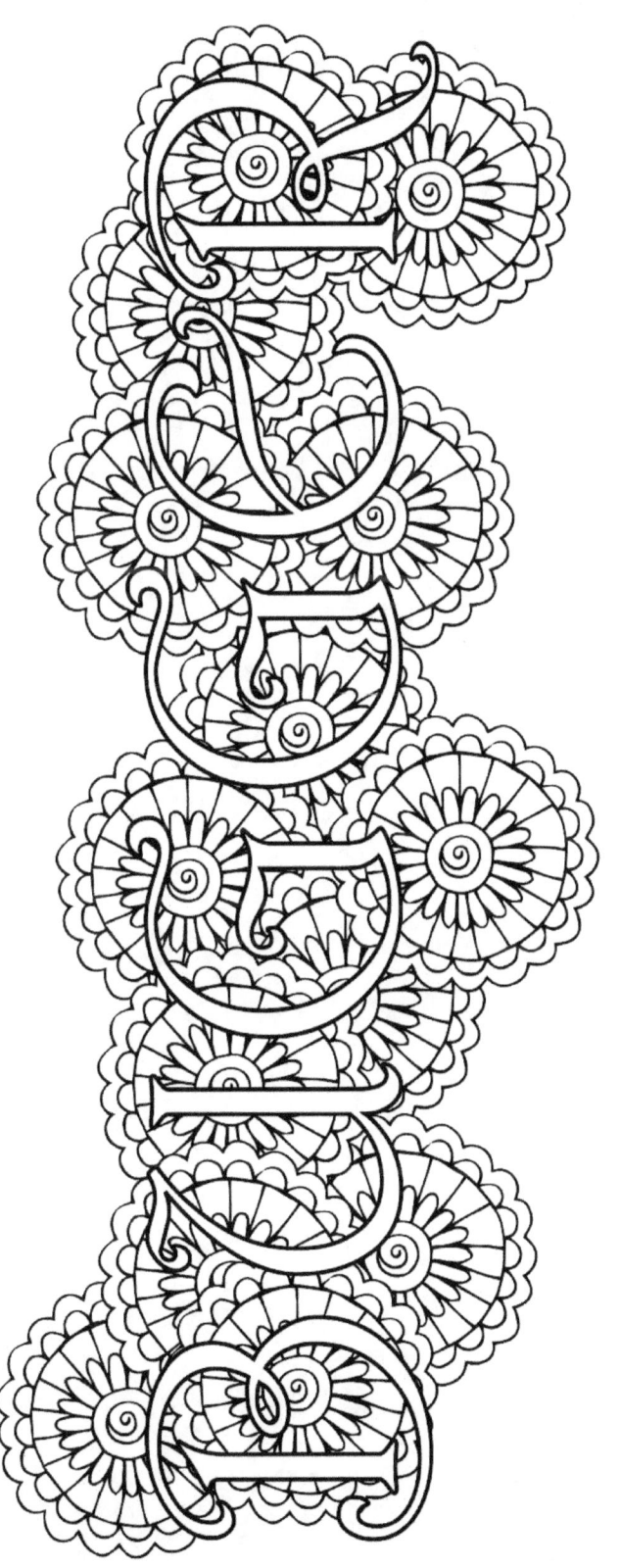

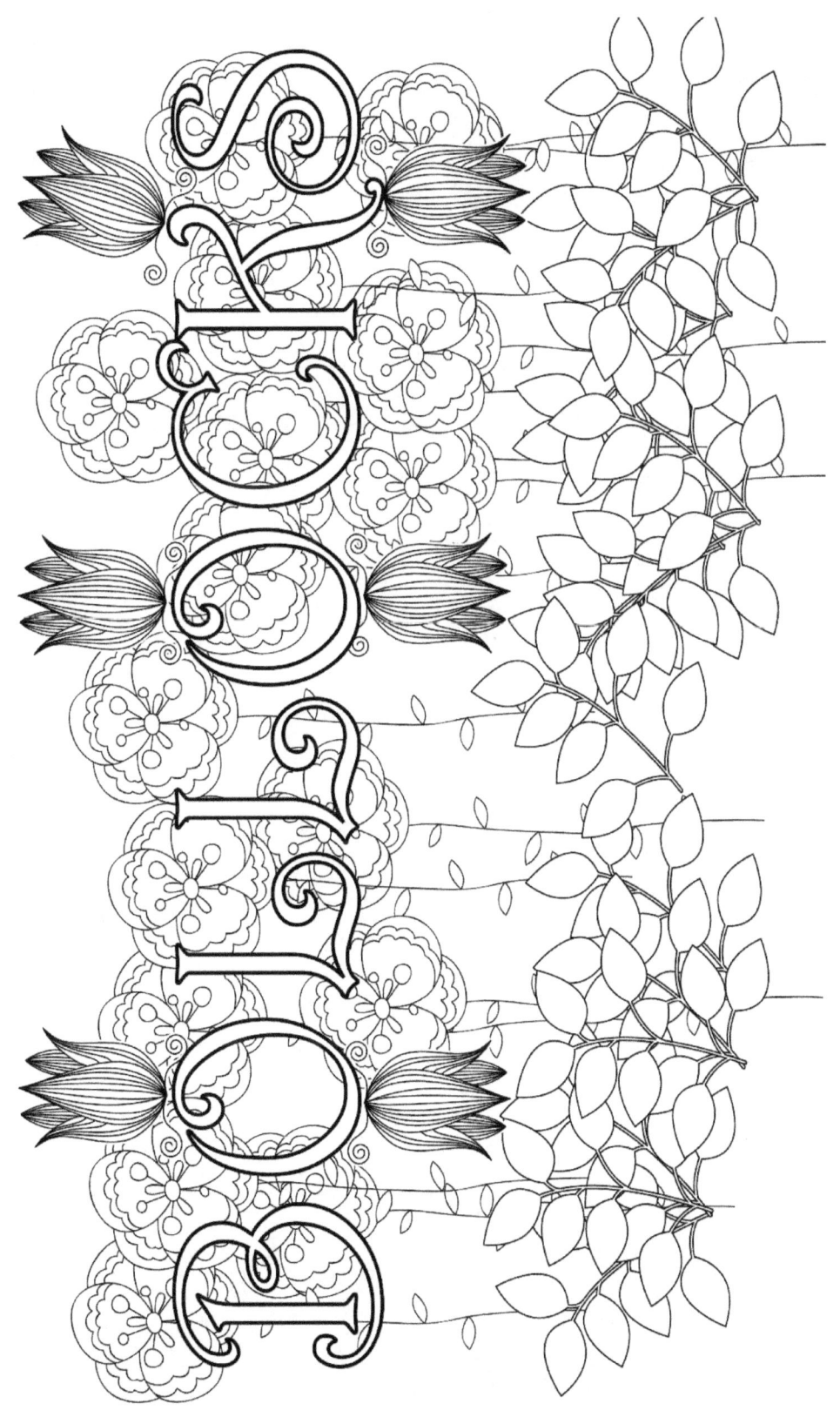

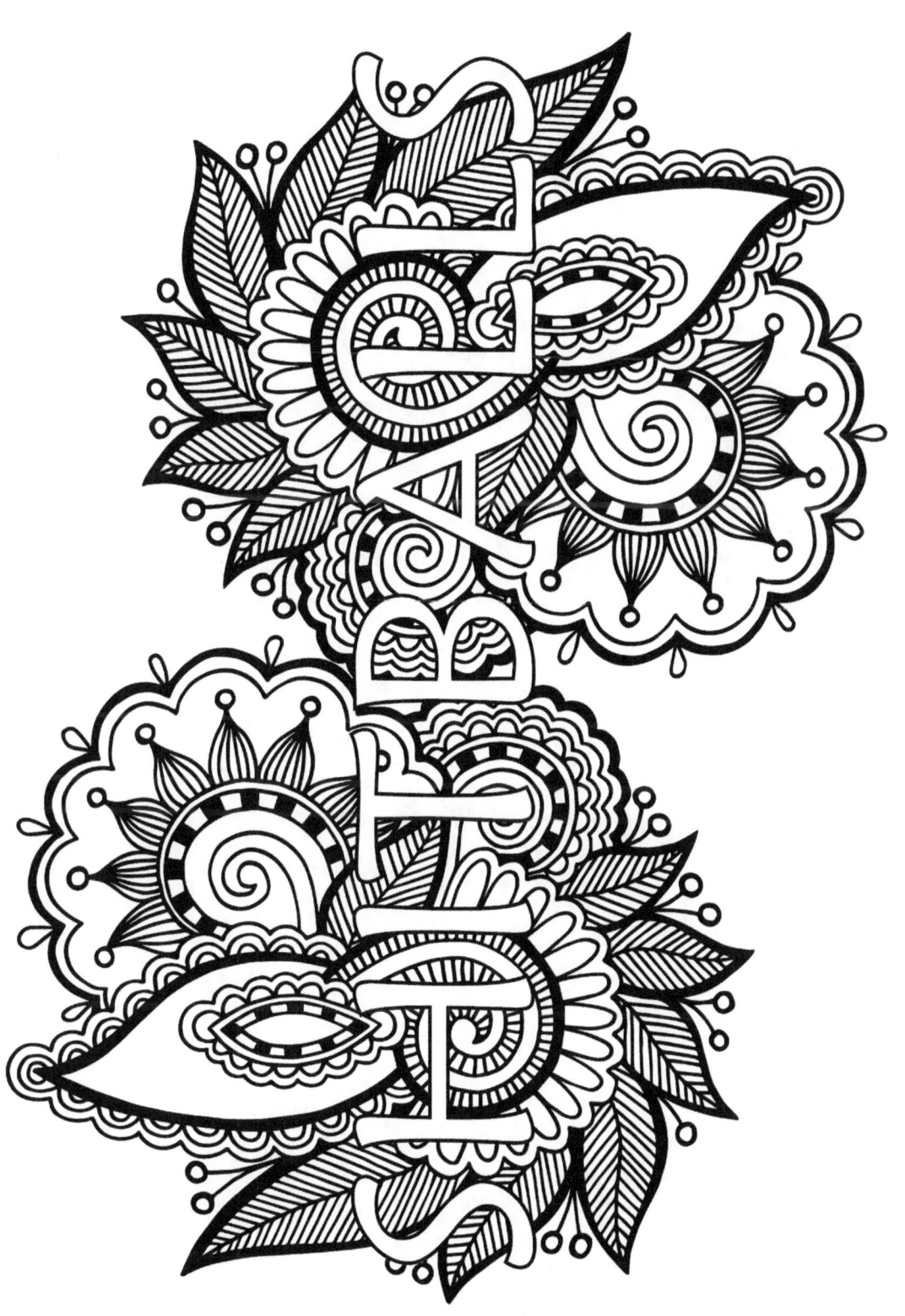

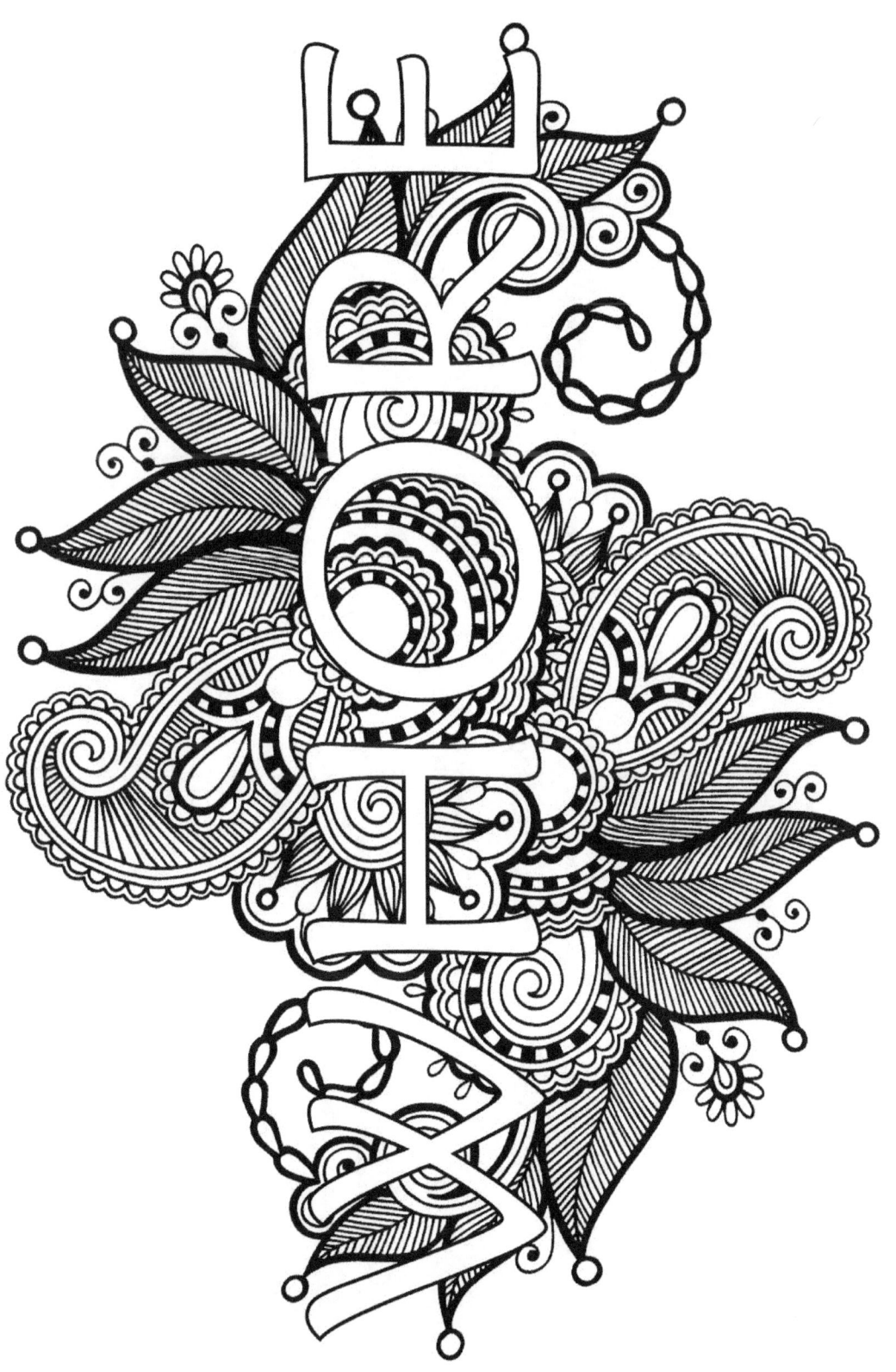

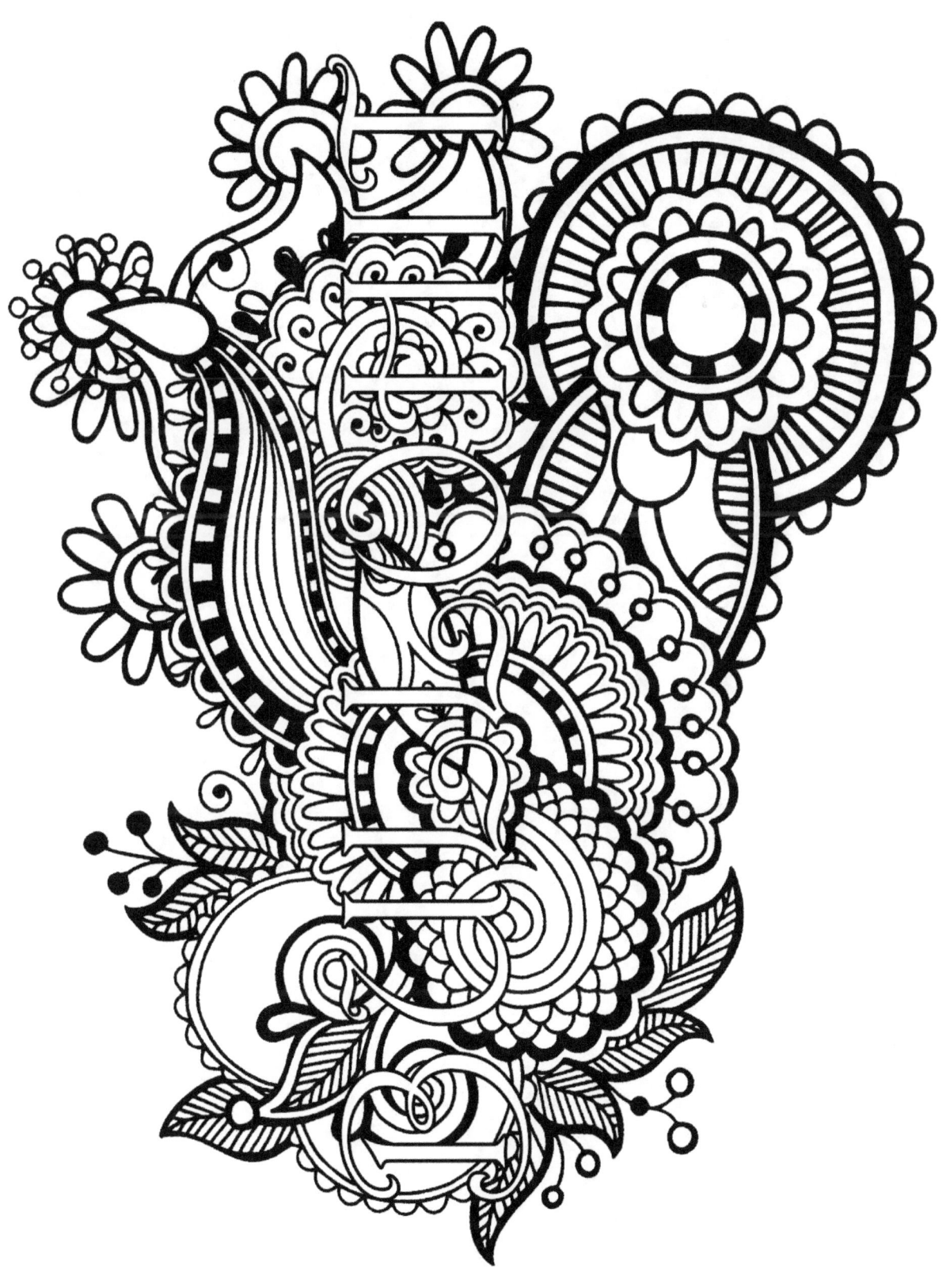

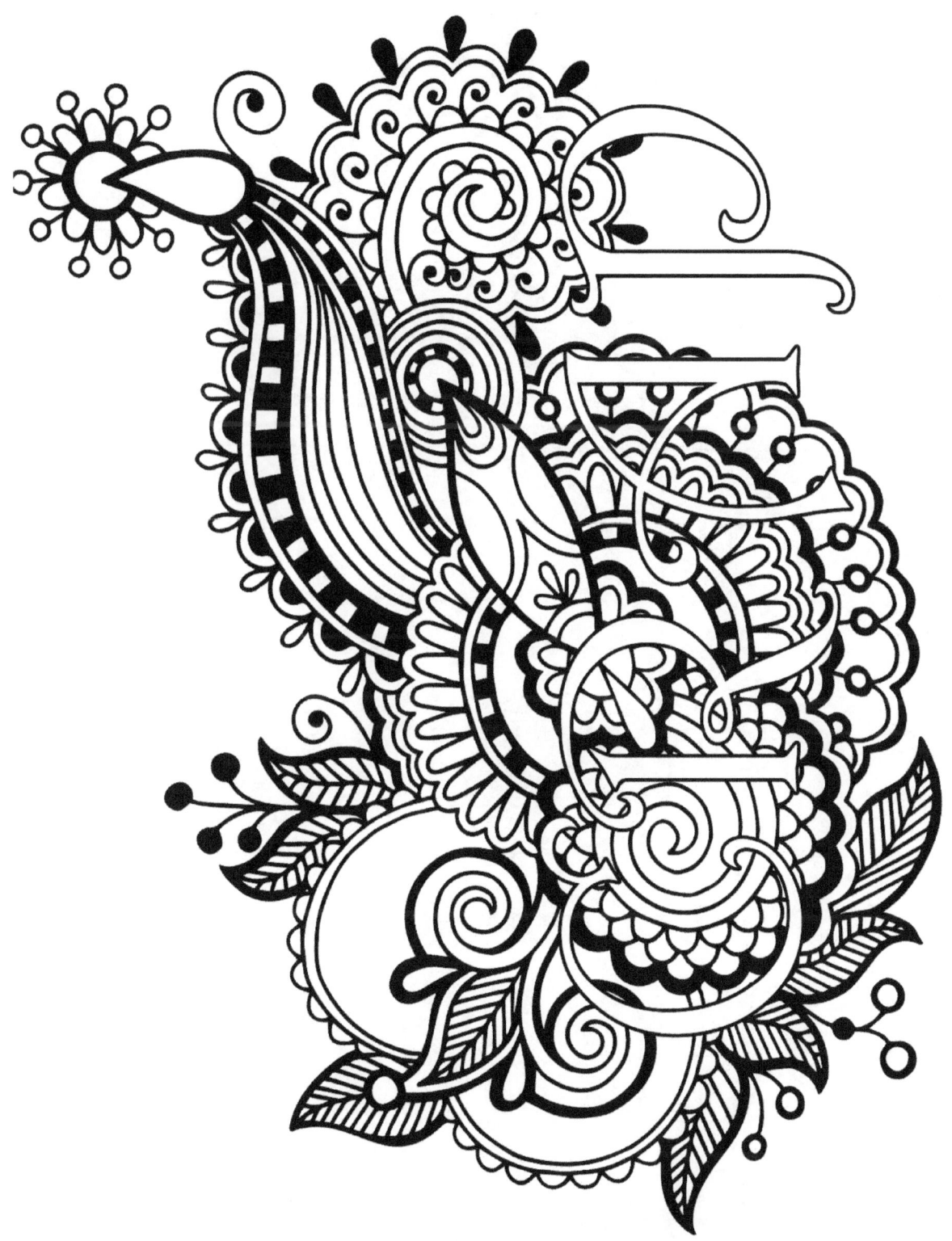

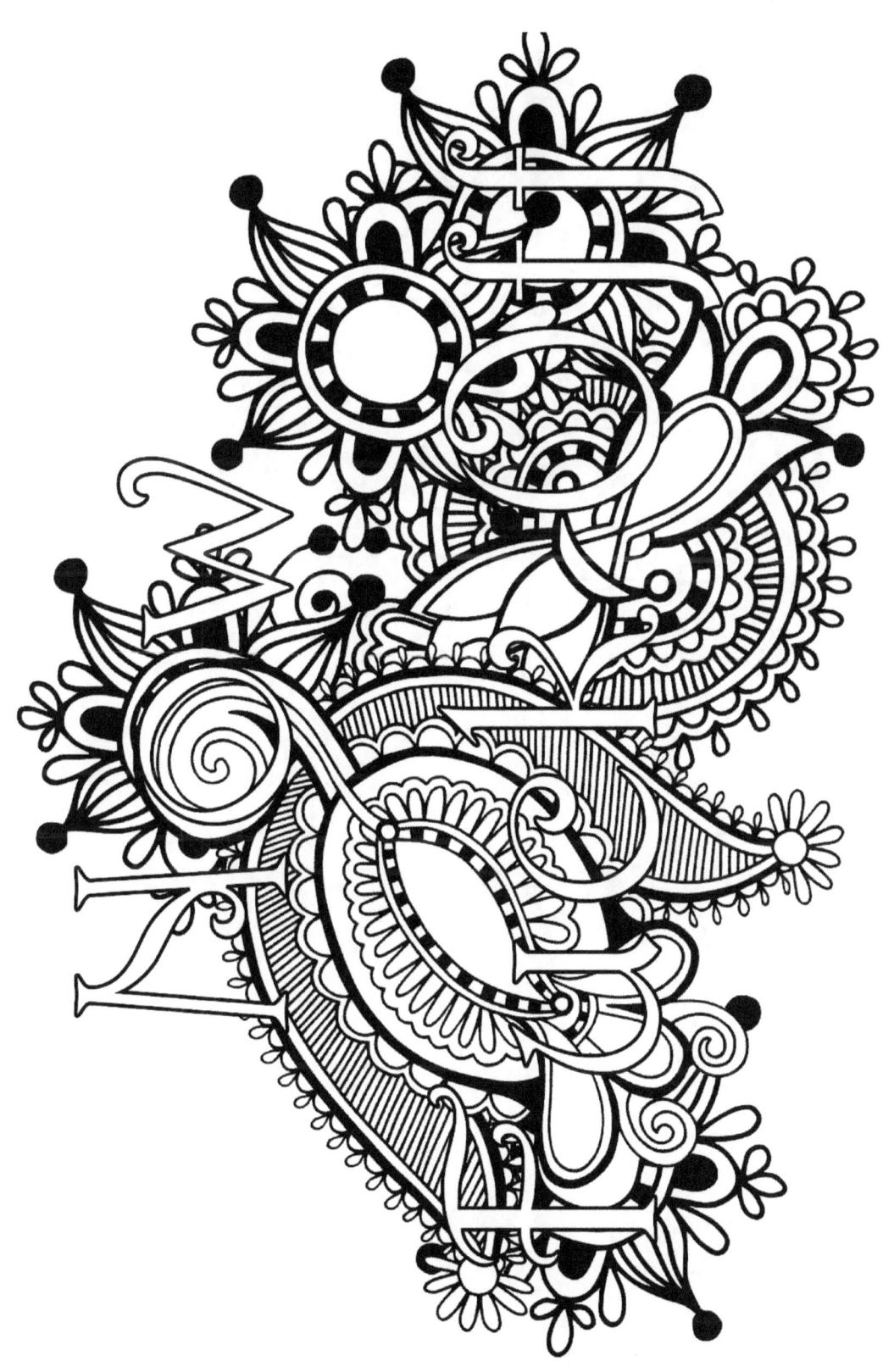

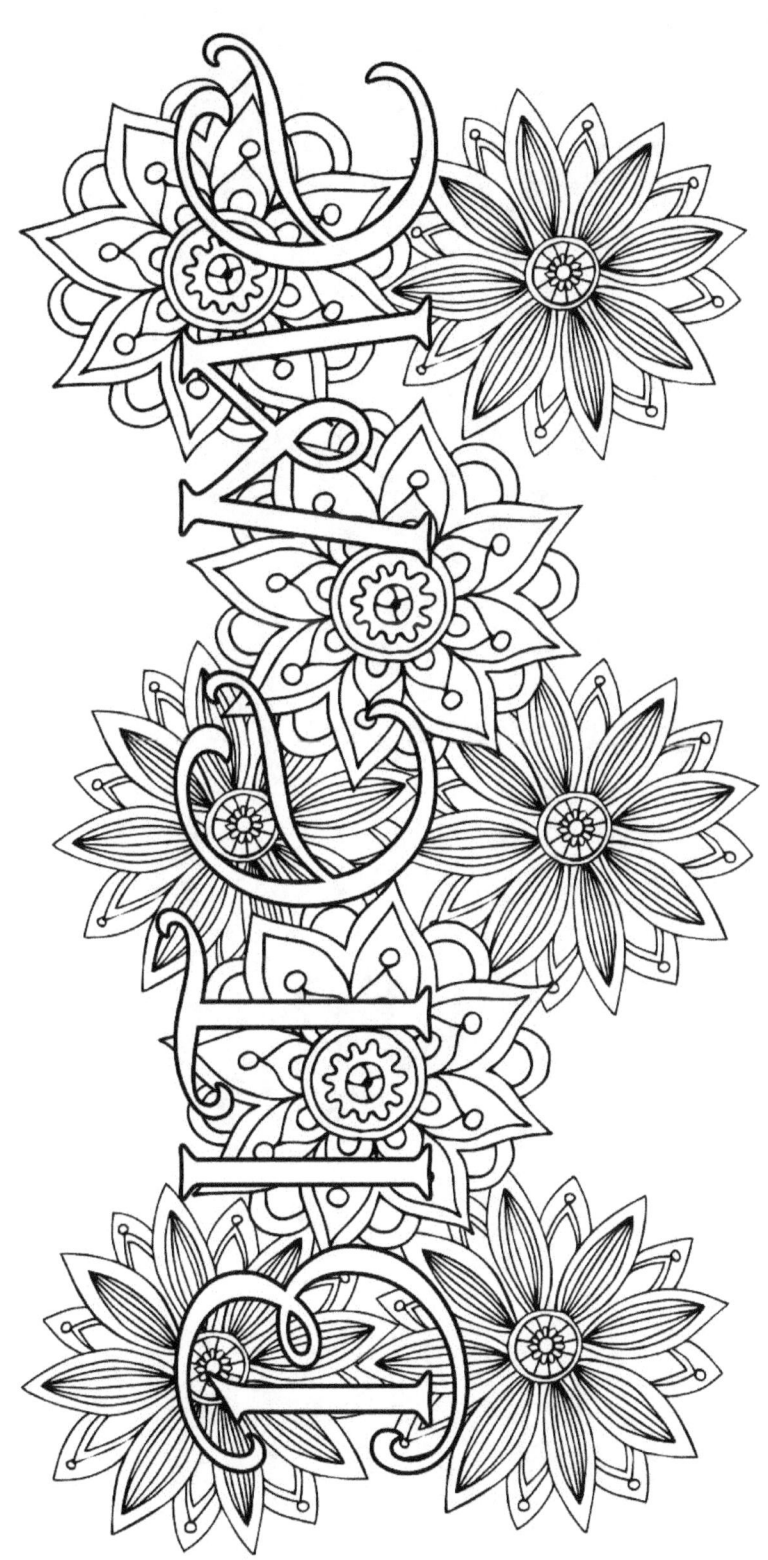

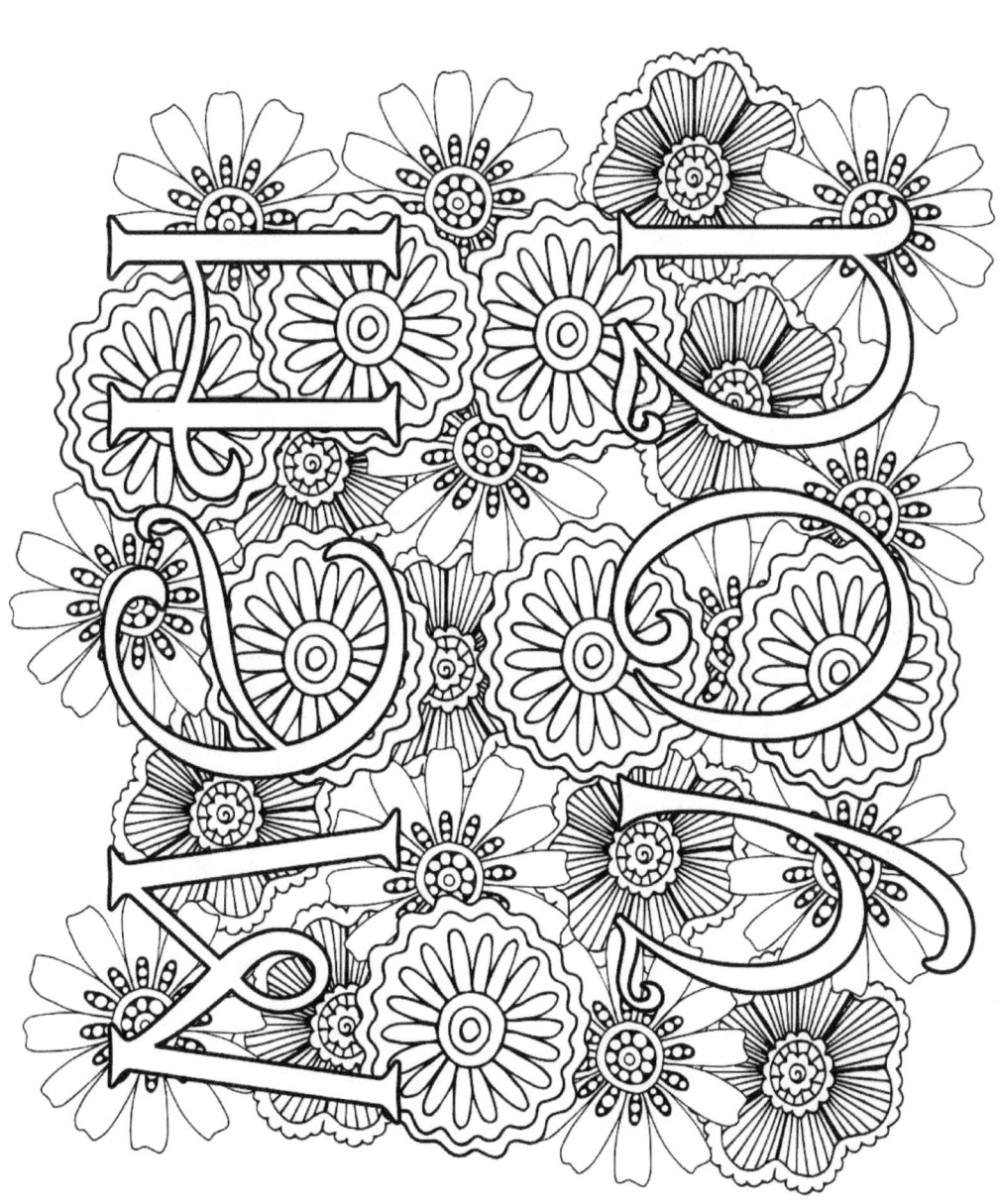

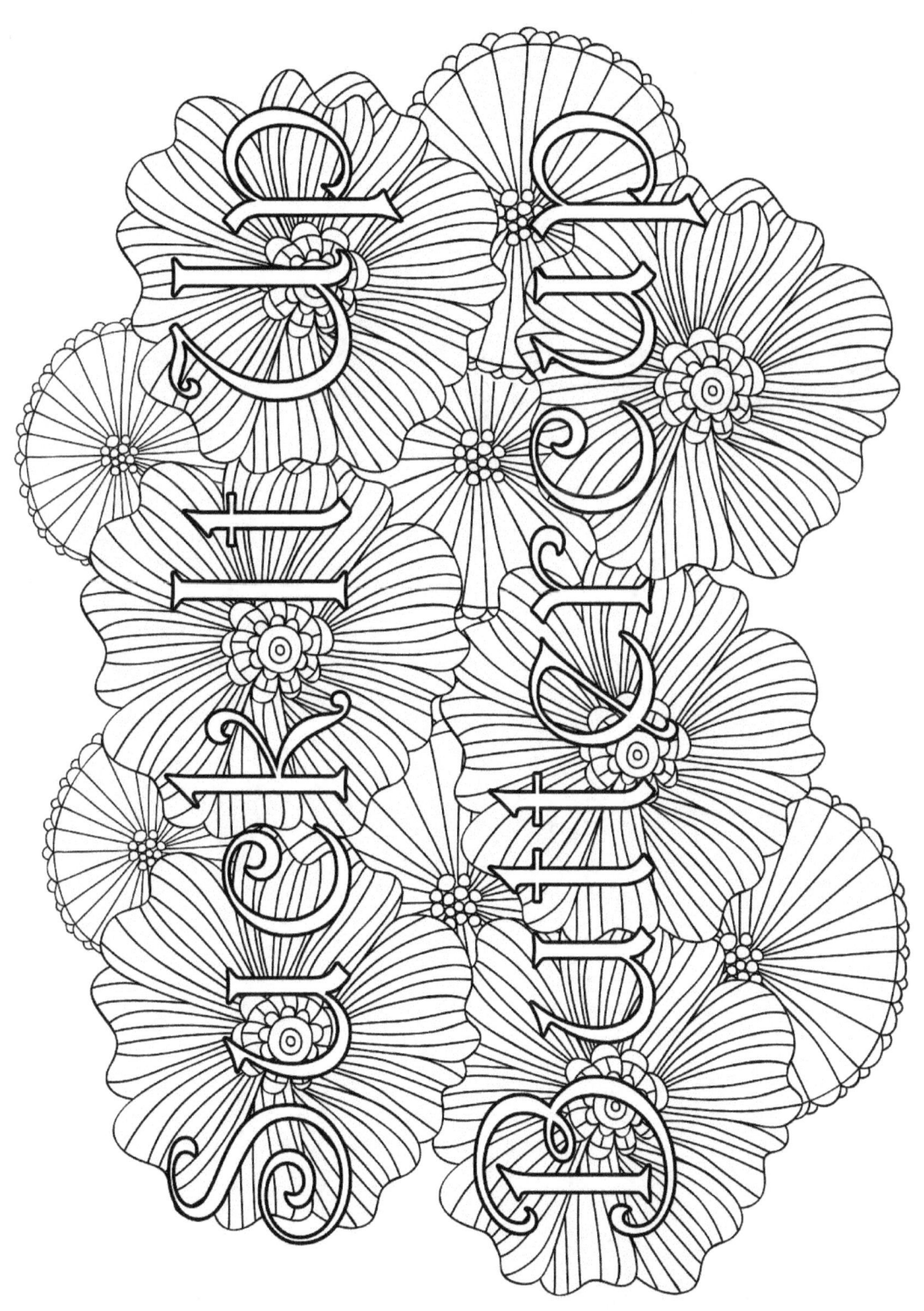

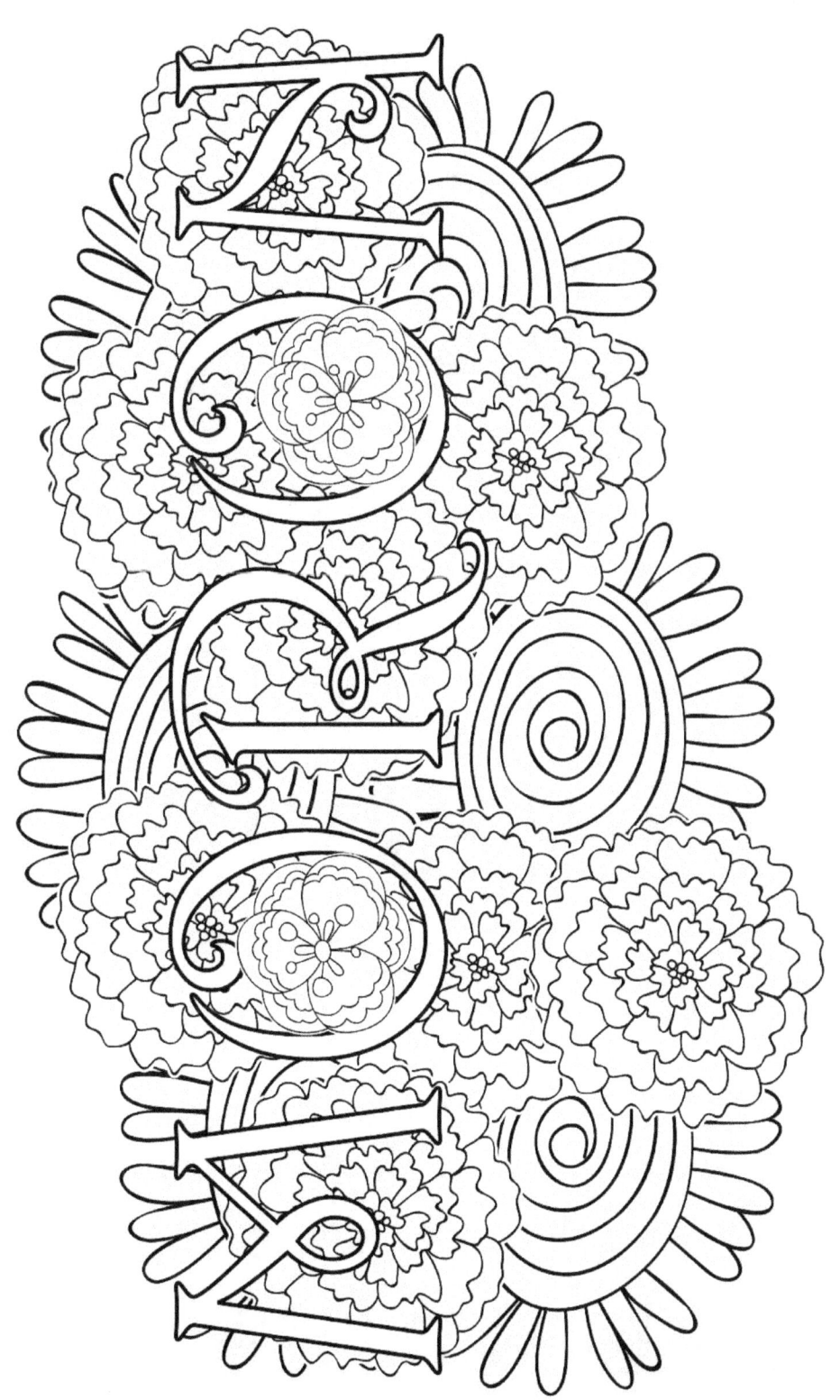

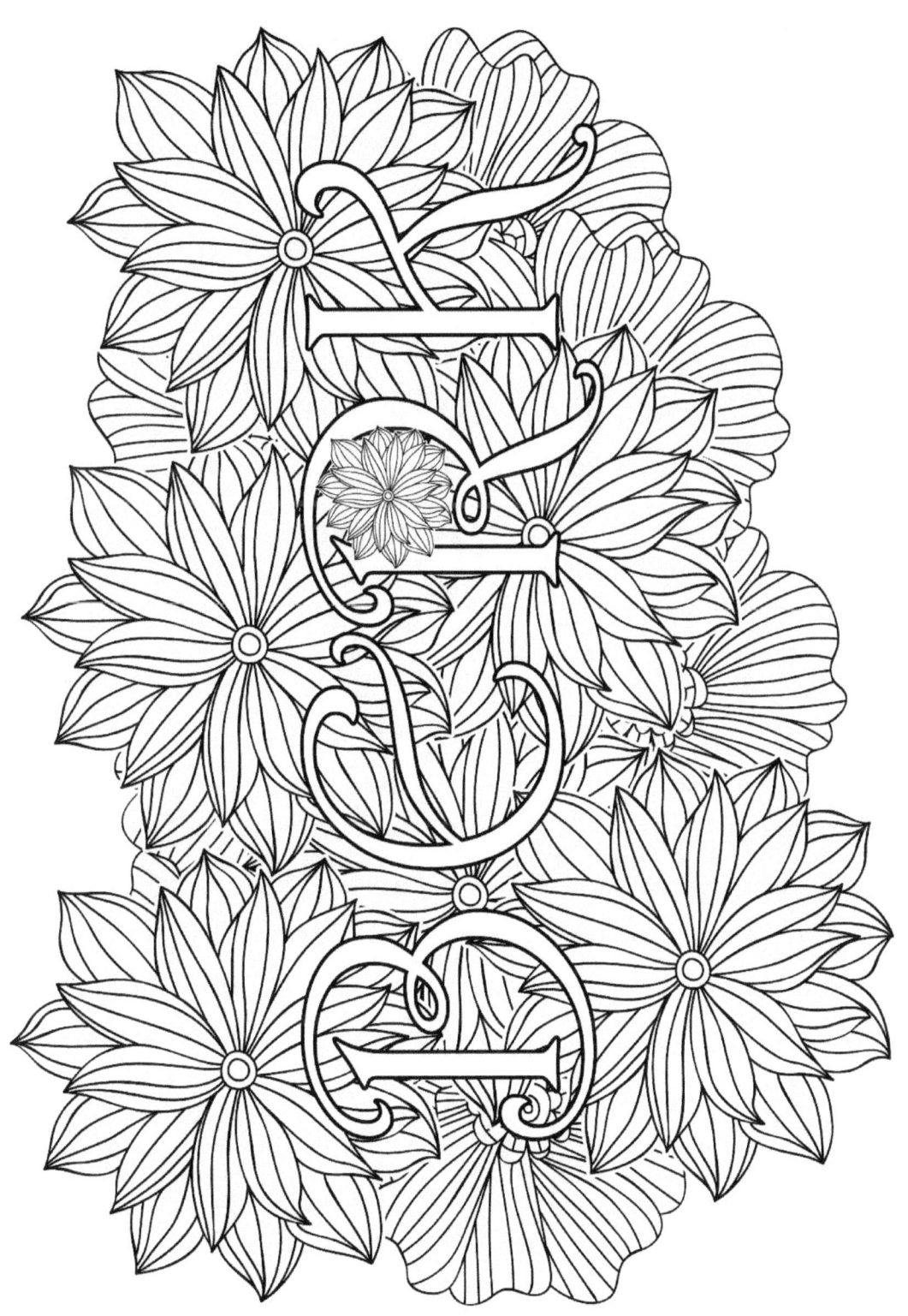

Thank You

Hope you've enjoyed your reading experience.

We here at Adult Coloring Book J. Kaiwell will always strive to deliver to you the highest quality guides.

So I'd like to thank you for supporting us and reading until the very end.

Before you go, would you mind leaving us a review on Amazon?

It will mean a lot to us and support us creating high quality guides for you in the future.

Thanks once again and here's where you can leave a review.

Get Free Ebook Coloring Page below

www.allcoloringbook.com/bonus

Warmly yours,

The Adult Coloring Book J. Kaiwell Team

www.ingramcontent.com/pod-product-compliance
Lightning Source LLC
Chambersburg PA
CBHW080629190526
45169CB00009B/3335